Dinosaurs

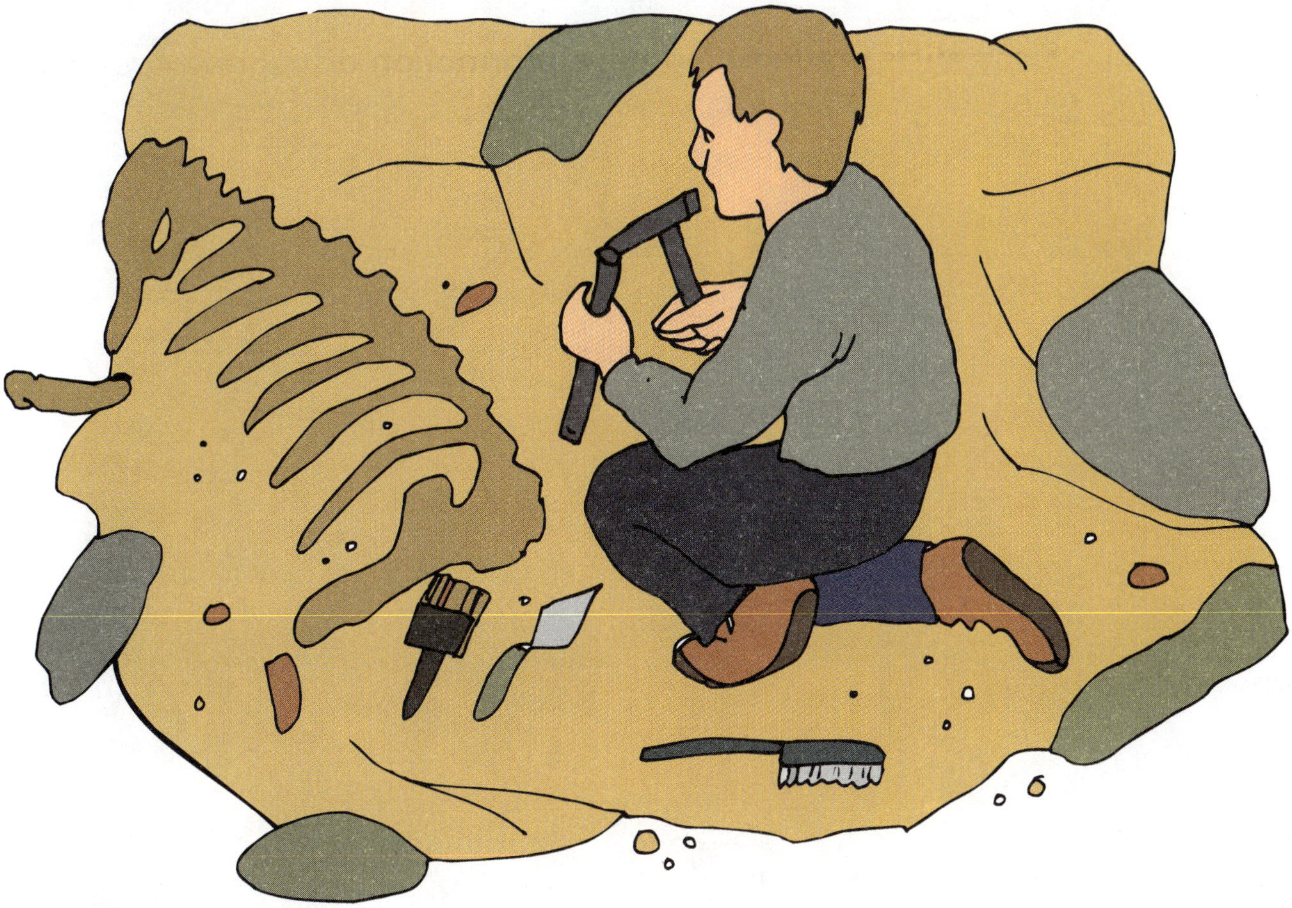

I'm a paleontologist. I study fossils to find out about life long ago. I've been working on this dig for weeks now. Today I discovered some new dinosaur bones. As I study these fossils I hope to answer some of my questions about dinosaurs.

A "fossil" is the hardened remains or print of an animal or plant that lived long ago.

Once many kinds of dinosaurs lived on the earth. There aren't any alive today, so how do we know they ever lived?

No people were alive at the same time as the dinosaurs. There are no paintings or books to tell us about them. We have to try to understand dinosaurs by studying the fossils we find.

We know a lot about the dinosaurs. We can tell how big the dinosaurs were, what type of food they ate, and when they lived. But there are still many questions.

What color were the dinosaurs?

Were they cold-blooded or warm-blooded?

Did they live alone or did they move in herds?

Did all meat-eaters hunt their prey or were some scavengers?

Did they take care of their babies or abandon their eggs?

What caused them to disappear? Did they all disappear?

Paleontologists and other scientists are beginning to answer some of these questions. Maybe someday they will be able to agree on the answers to all of these questions. But for now they must keep looking, digging, and studying.

Do you have your own questions about dinosaurs? Maybe you will find some of the answers in this book.

The Age of Dinosaurs

Dinosaur names can be difficult to say. If you need help, look on page 32.

Scientists have divided the long history of the earth into periods of time. The dinosaurs lived during four of these periods. Look at this chart to see when some of the dinosaurs lived. Don't forget, this was a long, long, long time ago.

The Age of Dinosaurs

Cretaceous Period (65 million years ago)	Today
Triceratops	no dinosaurs alive

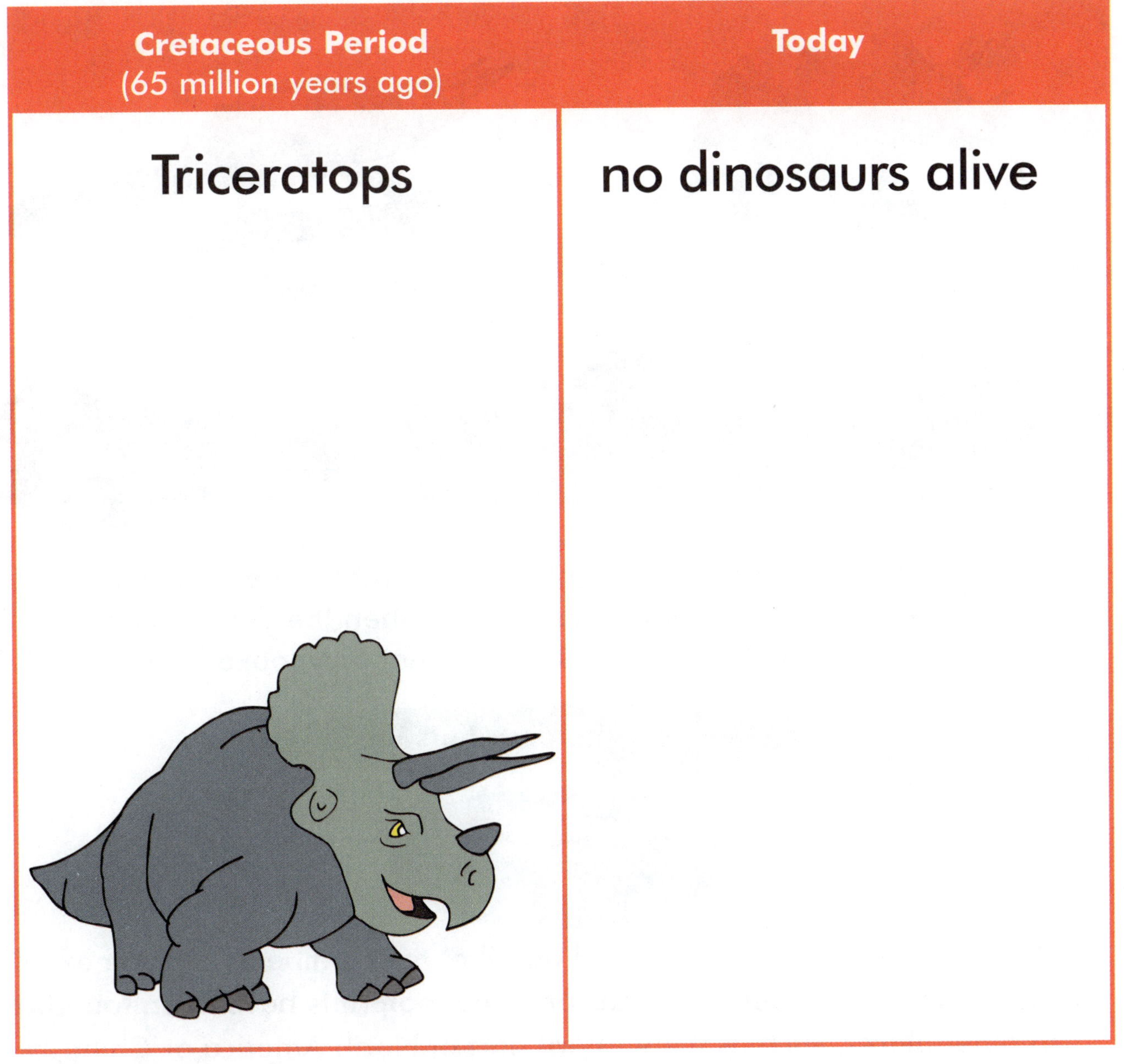

Quick Questions About Dinosaurs

What is a dinosaur?

Dinosaurs were reptiles that lived in prehistoric times. That was many millions of years ago.

Like the reptiles living today, dinosaurs had backbones and scaly skin. They laid eggs, and were cold-blooded.

ancient reptiles

reptiles today

How do we know dinosaurs lived?

Fossils of dinosaur bones, footprints, and teeth have been found and studied by scientists. The scientists can tell when the dinosaurs lived, where they lived, and some things about what they looked like.

Where did the dinosaurs live?

Dinosaur fossils have been found on all of the continents. In some places only a few teeth or bones or some footprints have been found. In other places, such as the western part of North America or China, large numbers of fossils have been discovered.

Fossils

What is a fossil?

Fossils are the hardened remains of animals or plants that lived long, long ago. Some dinosaur fossils are prints left after the animal parts decayed. There are fossils of whole skeletons and nests of dinosaur eggs. Bones, teeth, and footprints and prints of skin have all been found.

How is a dinosaur fossil made?

After the animal died, all of the soft parts decayed and disappeared. The hard parts like bones and teeth remained lying on the ground. Some of the bones were quickly covered with sand, mud, or water.

Over a long, long time minerals would seep in and take the place of the bone. What was left was a rock in the same shape as the bone. This rock is what we call a fossil.

Make Your Own Fossils

Parents: Your child will need a few supplies to do these activities. Self-hardening clay will make a longer-lasting print, but modeling clay can be used. Your help will be needed to mix the plaster of Paris for the fossil bones project.

Fossil Prints

You need:

- clay
- a leaf, bone, or shell
- rolling pin

Steps:

1. Roll out the clay.
2. Put your leaf, bone, or shell into the clay. Press it down with your hand. Take it off the clay.
3. Let the clay dry.

Extra:

Dinosaurs left behind fossil prints of their feet. You can make a print of your foot or hand using the same steps. Roll out the clay, press your hand or foot in it. Take your foot away and let the clay dry.

Make Fossil Bones

These will not really be fossils. It would take millions of years to turn your bones into fossils. This just shows you how it might happen.

Fossil Bones

You need:

- plaster of Paris
- water
- stick for stirring
- measuring cup
- large milk carton
- bones (clean chicken or beef bones)

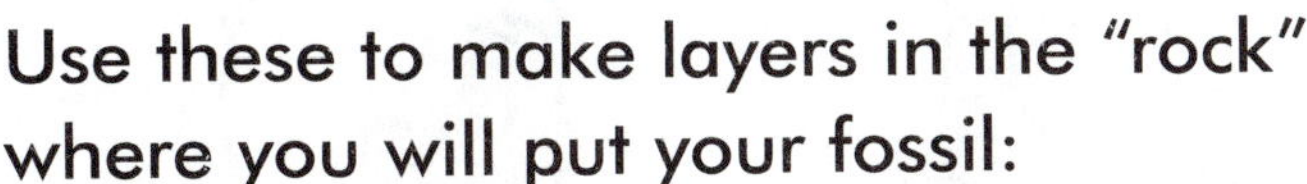

Use these to make layers in the "rock" where you will put your fossil:

- fine sand
- coarse sand
- small gravel
- fine bark chips (or you can use just sand if that is all you have)

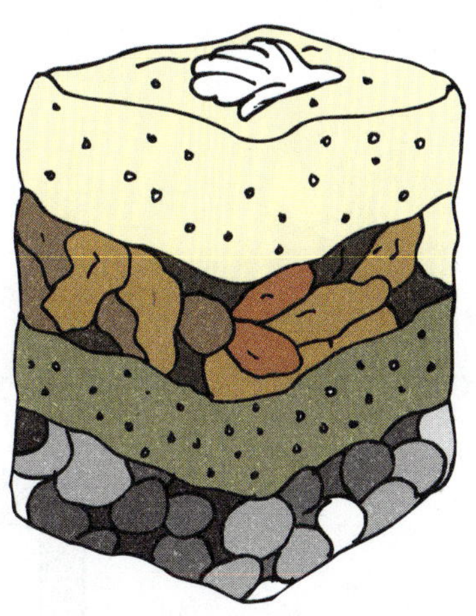

Steps:

1. Cut the top off of the milk carton.
2. Put a layer of each of these in the carton: fine sands, coarse sand, gravel, bark chips. After your carton is half full, put in your bones or shells. Cover them with more layers of your materials. You may make more than one layer of a material.
3. Mix the plaster of Paris. Pour it into the milk carton until all the layers are covered. (Lift the carton and tap it on the table to help the plaster fill in all the spaces.) Let it sit until the plaster is dry.
4. Tear away the milk carton. Look at the layers. Do you see any of your "fossils" sticking out?
5. Break open your "rock" and find your fossils.

Be a Paleontologist

Parents: Your child will need the clean bones of a chicken to do this exploration. You can get a chicken head and feet at your grocery meat counter.

Finding dinosaur bones is only the first step. The paleontologist has to study the bones. One job is to try to fit the pieces together. You can try this yourself.

First you need bones. Ask your parents to save the bones the next time you have chicken for dinner. You will need their help to clean the bones.

1. Scrape off any scraps of meat.

2. Boil the bones for an hour in soapy water.

3. Rinse the bones in clear hot water. Set them out to dry.

Now comes the interesting part. Try to lay the bones out in the correct places. Look at each bone. Ask yourself "What kind of bone is this?" "Where should it go?" Good luck! Remember, scientists don't always get it right the first time.

What Color Were the Dinosaurs?

Bones and teeth are the parts of the dinosaur most often found. These do not show the dinosaur's color. Sometimes a print of dinosaur skin is found. It shows if the dinosaur was smooth or bumpy, but it doesn't show its color.

So no one knows what color dinosaurs really were. Maybe they were shades of green and brown so they could hide among the trees in swamps and jungles. But maybe they were bright colors or had colorful stripes and dots. No one knows. So you can make your dinosaurs any color you like!

Color these dinosaurs.

Were All Dinosaurs Huge?

Most dinosaurs you see in movies or read about in books were huge. While many dinosaurs were enormous, some were very small. Compsognathus was about the size of a chicken.

How Tall? How Long?

Some dinosaurs were so big it is difficult to imagine how tall or how long they really were. Other dinosaurs were very small. Use string and a measuring tape to see how big or how small these dinosaurs were.

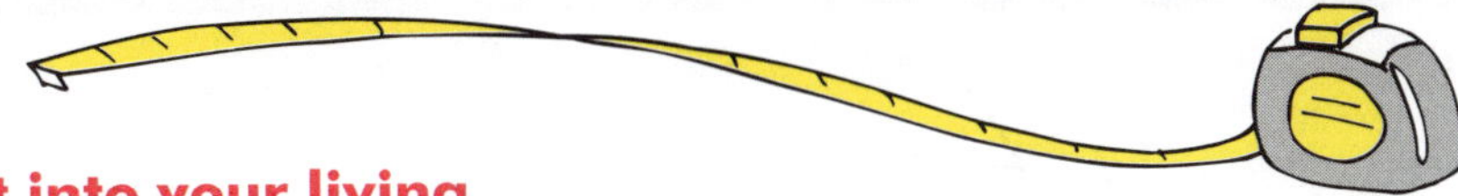

Would a triceratops fit into your living room?

1 Triceratops was about 25 feet (7.5 meters) long. Measure a piece of string that long. Stretch the string the longest way in your living room. Could a triceratops fit into the room?

2 Triceratops was nine and a half feet (3 meters) tall. Measure a piece of string that long. Ask an adult to help you see if the string reaches from the ceiling to the floor. Could a triceratops stand up in your living room?

What can you find in your house that is as tall as these dinosaurs? (Sizes can be approximate)

1. Compsognathus
   1 foot tall (30 cm tall) ______________________

2. Velociraptor
   6 feet tall, (180 cm tall) ______________________

3. Protoceratops
   2 1/2 feet tall (45 cm tall) ______________________

What Did Dinosaurs Eat?

Scientists can make a good guess by looking at the shape of the dinosaur's teeth.

Meat-eaters usually have teeth with sharp points and jagged edges. This helps them tear up the meat.

Plant-eaters had teeth that were smooth and flat on top for grinding plants.

Scientists think that some plant-eating dinosaurs didn't have flat surfaces on their teeth. Iguanodon had jagged teeth, but they were not sharp like the teeth of a meat-eater.

Some large plant-eaters have been found with small stones in the middle of their skeletons. Scientists think they may have swallowed the stones to help grind up their food. This is what modern birds do.

Are you a plant-eater, a meat-eater, or are you both? Circle the types of foods you eat.

How Did They Move?

Some moved on two legs. Others moved on four legs.

The meat-eaters usually had short front legs and longer back legs. They moved around on the two back legs. Their tails were held out to balance their heavy heads and chests.

Plant-eaters usually had four legs about the same size. They walked around on all four legs. Some were able to raise up on two legs to reach for food up in trees.

Circle the plant-eaters.
Underline the meat-eaters.

Other Prehistoric Reptiles

Not all prehistoric reptiles were dinosaurs. The pterosaurs were flying reptiles. They were relatives of the dinosaurs, but they were not dinosaurs.

Another group of dinosaur relatives lived in the sea. These sea reptiles swam in the water like fish.

Dinosaur Life Cycle

Scientists think dinosaurs laid eggs just like modern reptiles do. Fossil eggs and nests have been found in several places around the world. Some of the fossil eggs contained skeletons of baby dinosaurs.

Life cycle of protoceratops

Protoceratops is the first dinosaur for which fossils have been found that show every stage of life. Scientists found potato-shaped eggs laying in nests. The bowl-shaped nests were dug in the sand. The eggs were laid in two or three circles inside the nest. There were also "hatchling" fossils and fossils of adult dinosaurs in the same place.

Cut out these pictures. Paste them in order in the boxes on page 18. Write what each picture shows.

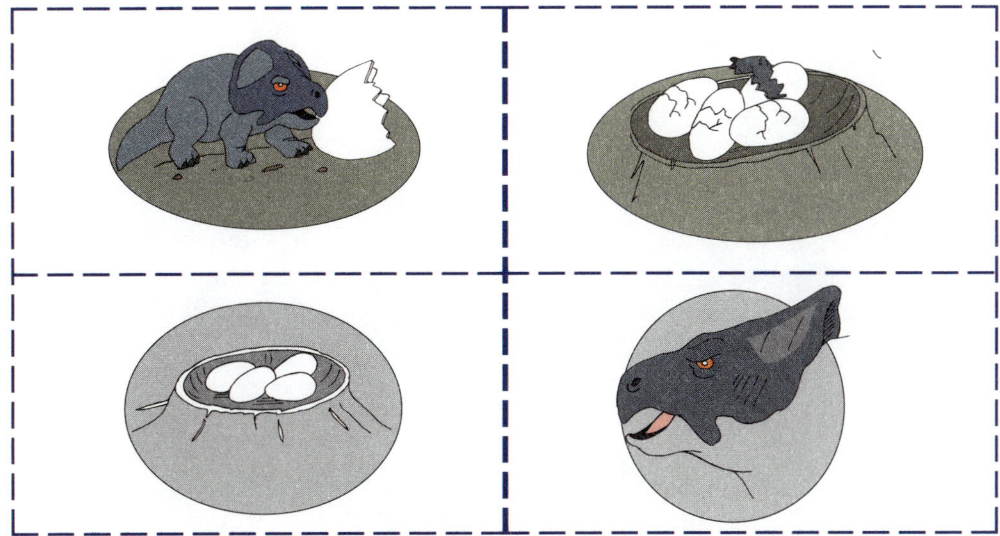

Life Cycle of Protoceratops

Why Did the Dinosaurs Disappear?

Scientists do not agree on what caused dinosaurs to become extinct. They have come up with many ideas, but there is no proof that any one idea is what really happened.

There is some evidence that only the large dinosaurs became extinct. Some scientists believe the small dinosaurs did not become extinct. Over a long period of time they gradually changed into animals that live today.

Most scientists now think that the dinosaurs died because of changes in the climate. The climate became too hot and plants died. Without food, the plant-eaters died. The meat-eaters then had less food to eat. After a time the weather became very cold, and the remaining large dinosaurs died.

What scientists don't agree on is what caused this change. Was it a giant comet hitting the earth? Were there eruptions of large volcanoes? No one knows. Scientists are still trying to find the answer.

Have All the Dinosaurs Disappeared?

Some scientists think that the small meat-eating dinosaurs are the ancestors of modern birds.

The skeletons of the little dinosaur compsognathus and the first bird archaeopteryx look very much alike. The biggest difference is feathers. Archaeopteryx had them. Compsognathus didn't.

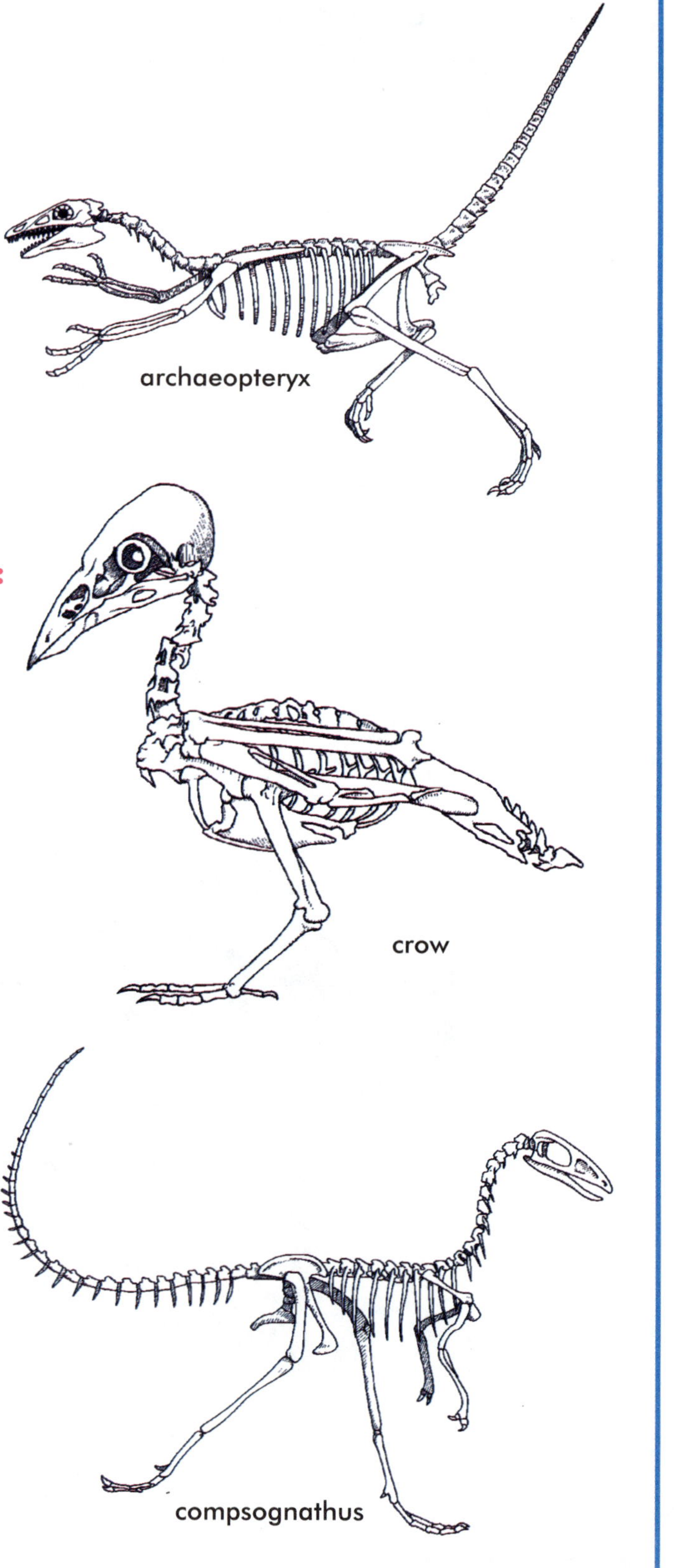

How the small dinosaurs were like birds:

1. Their legs went straight down from their hips.

2. They had 3 toes that pointed forward.
   The middle toe was the long-est.

3. Many of their bones were like the bones of modern birds.

What do you think? Maybe you will grow up to be a paleontologist and solve this mystery.

3-D Dinosaurs

Here are three different kinds of dinosaurs you can make.

Clay Dinosaur

Take a lump of clay.
Pinch and pull the clay
to make your dinosaur.

Aluminum Foil Dinosaurs

Crumple sheet of
aluminum foil into the
shape of a dinosaur.
Use permanent marking
pens to add eyes and
other features.

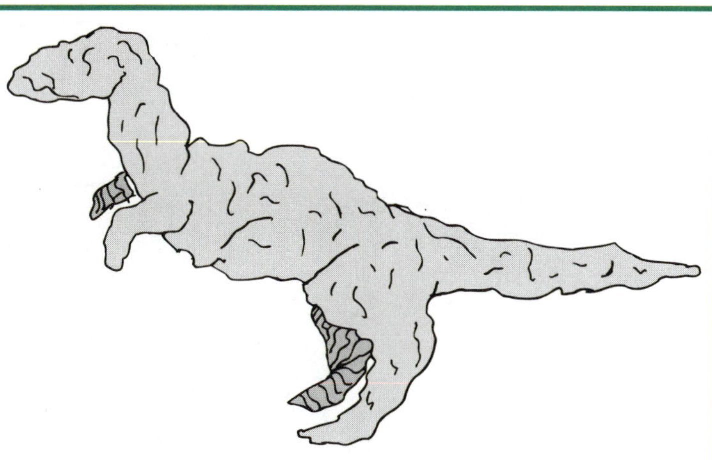

Dinosaur Skeletons

Use pipe cleaners to
make a skeleton.
Twist the pieces of pipe
cleaners together.

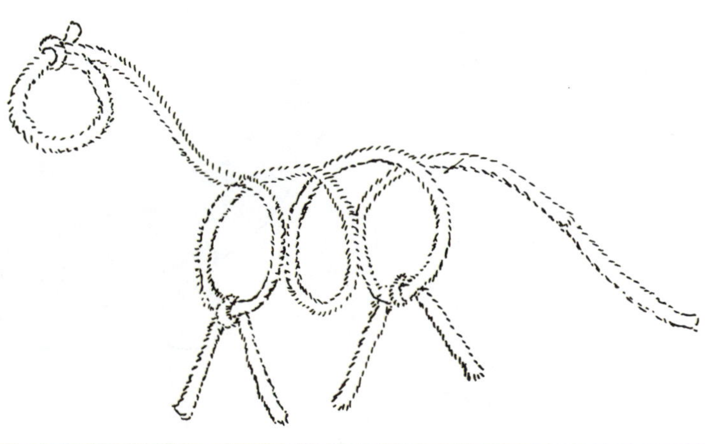

Draw a Dinosaur

Follow these steps to draw a dinosaur.

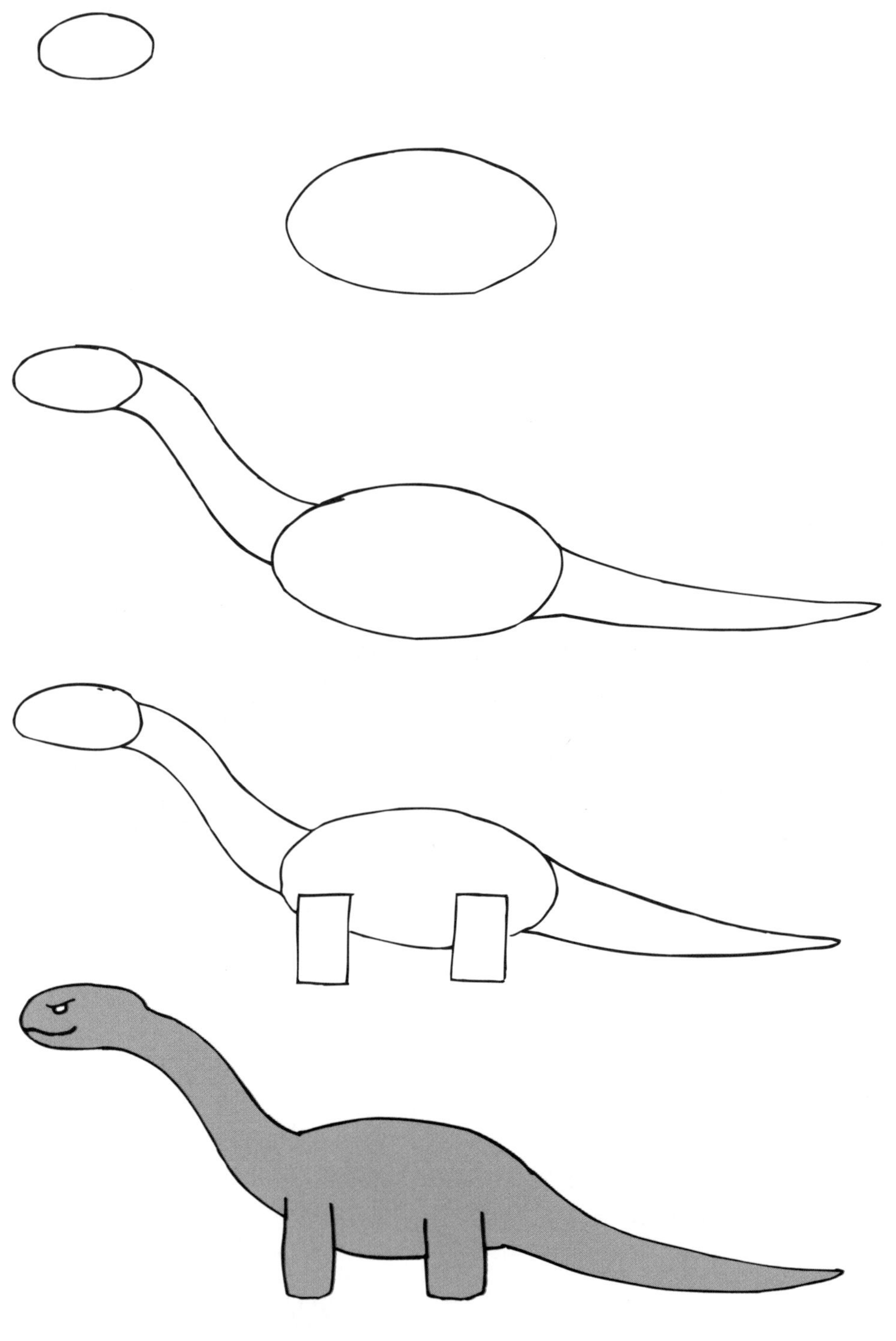

Dinosaur Jigsaw Puzzle

Cut pieces apart. Paste them to another sheet of paper to make a picture.

Dinosaur Riddles

1. We use sharp pointed teeth to eat our food. Who are we?

2. I have three large horns on my head. Which dinosaur am I?

3. We are the clues scientists use to find out about dinosaurs. What are we?

4. I was the first flying animal with feathers. Who am I?

5. I am the scientist who studies fossils. Who am I?

6. I am a prehistoric flying reptile. Who am I?

Word Box

archaeopteryx	paleontologist	meat-eaters
fossils	pteranodon	triceratops

Dinosaur Cards

Cut apart the cards on pages 27 and 29. Here are some things you can do with the cards to help you learn more about dinosaurs.

1. Put the cards in a stack. Take one at a time and try to name the dinosaur. Turn the card over to see if you are right.

2. Read the back of the cards to learn facts about dinosaurs.

3. Sort the cards in these ways.

   a. Put all of the meat-eaters in one stack. Put the plant-eaters in another stack.

   b. Find the card that does not show a dinosaur. What kind of animal is it?

   c. Put the cards in a line with the smallest dinosaur in front and the biggest dinosaur in back.

3. Pick one dinosaur. Go to the library and find out more information about it.

4. You will need a friend to play with you.

   Show a picture card. Tell something (true or made up) about the dinosaur.

   Ask your friend. "Is this true?" If your friend answers right, give the card to him/her. If your friend is wrong, you keep the card.

   Now switch. Your friend shows you a card and says something about the dinosaur. You decide if the statement is true.

Protoceratops

was the size of a large pig. It was about 6 feet (1.8 meters) long and very heavy. Its body was covered in bony armor. It was small enough to hide in the bushes if danger was near. It was a plant-eater. Protoceratops had sharp teeth and strong jaw muscles for tearing and chewing tough leaves.

Tyrannosaurus

was a huge meat-eating dinosaur. It was 50 feet (15 meters) long. When it ran, it held out its long tail to balance its huge head. It had long sharp teeth and claws. It had large strong back legs, but very short front legs. It was big, but not very fast.

Apatosaurus

was a large plant-eating dinosaur. It had a long neck and a long tail. It was 75 feet (23 meters) long. It had a small head and big feet and legs. It was a plant-eater. Its size and tough skin were its protection.

Compsognathus

was a very small dinosaur. It was about the size of a chicken. It ran along on two bird-like legs. It had hollow bones like most birds. It was a deadly hunter with sharp teeth. It probably ate insects and small reptiles and mammals.

Triceratops

was the biggest horned dinosaur. It was over 25 feet (7.5 meters) long and very heavy. It was a plant-eater. It could snip off tree branches with its sharp beak and chop them up with scissor-like teeth. It had no real enemies. Its horns, frill, and tough skin protected it.

Stegosaurus

was about the size of an elephant. It had two rows of leaf-shaped bony plates running down its back and onto its tail. Its long, heavy tail had four large spikes. It walked on all four legs, but could rear up on its hind legs to feed in the trees. Its teeth show that it was a plant-eater.

Plesiosaurus

wasn't a dinosaur. It was a prehistoric reptile that lived in the sea. It was 10 feet (3 meters) long and had a long snake-like neck, a barrel-shaped body, and a small head. It swam with its long paddle-like legs. It used its long neck to search for food below the water's surface. It ate small fish and other sea animals.

Ankylosaurus

was about 25 feet (7.5 meters) long. It had thick skin covered with bony plates. It had short spikes coming out of the side of its body. Its tail was short, thick, and had a club at the end. It looked dangerous, but it was a plant-eater.

Crossword Puzzle

Across

2. reptiles that lived long, long ago
4. these are found in dinosaur nests
6. the parts of a skeleton
7. these tell what food dinosaurs ate

Down

1. these are all that remain of dinosaurs
3. dinosaurs were this kind of animal
5. _____-eaters had sharp pointed teeth

Word Box

bones	meat
dinosaur	reptile
eggs	teeth
fossils	

Pronunciation Key

Allosaurus	(AL uh sawr us)
Anchisaurus	(ANG kee sawr us)
Ankylosaurus	(ang KILE uh sawr us)
Apatosaurus	(ah PAT uh sawr us)
Archaeopteryx	(ar kee OP ter ix)
Brachiosaurus	(BRAK ee uh sawr us)
Coelophysis	(see lo FISE iss)
Compsognathus	(komp so NAY thus)
Diplodocus	(dih PLOD uh kus)
Elasmosaurus	(ee LAZ muh sawr us)
Lambeosaurus	(LAM be uh sawr us)
Parasaurolophus	(par ah sawr OL uh fus)
Plateosaurus	(PLAY tee uh sawr us)
Plesiosaurus	(PLEE zee uh sawr us)
Protoceratops	(pro toe SAIR uh tops)
Pteranodon	(tair AN o don)
Rhamphorhynchus	(ram fo RINK us)
Stegosaurus	(STEG uh sawr us)
Struthiomimus	(strooth ee uh MY mus)
Triceratops	(try SAIR uh tops)
Tyrannosaurus	(tye RAN uh sawr us)
Velociraptor	(veh loss ih RAP tor)